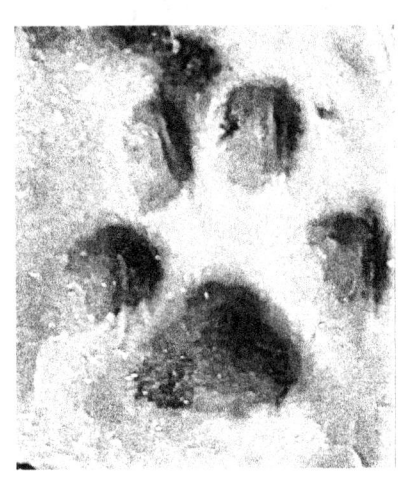

Foxey's Pawtograph

Copyright 2023 A Drop From Eden

All rights Reserved

No part of this publication may be reproduced, distributed, or transmitted in any form

9781958189160

"It's impossible to forget something that gave you so much to remember."

This book is dedicated to the best friend girl could ever hope for.

"No longer by my side, but forever in my heart."

Foxey Lady Patterson

1/29/01-1/26/13

My mommy and I have been on many fabulous adventures, but our story didn't start that way.

You see mommy was paraplegic meaning her legs don't work. And the man that had me was a breeder so all he cared about was making money not of us having good homes.

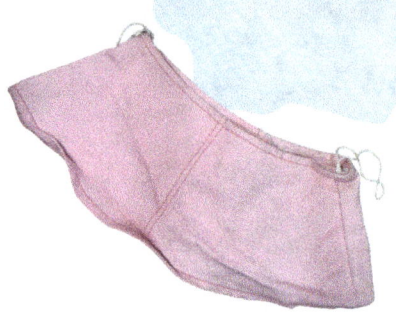

The man had already sold my siblings, but no one wanted me because I was different. I didn't like playing fetch, tug-a-war or any of the things most dogs like. I enjoyed playing dress-up, and loved to talk.

The breeder man told me I needed to fit in, but I refused.

He said, I was too old to be with him and "I was going to the pound if I didn't have a home by the weekend. This made me have nightmares that I was locked in a small dark cage and could not be me.

The next day the man took me to an auction, but before he could auction me off, my mommy found me. The breeder man told my mom. "You don't want her. She will be too much work for you." "I have a puppy at home that's better suited for you."

Mommy said no. You see, she was different too. She told the man. "I have been told my entire life I wasn't capable of being who I am because I'm in a wheelchair". We are a perfect match." With that, mommy took me home, but this was just the beginning.

When we arrived home, I saw mommy already had everything I needed delivered. I had rhinestone food bowls, lots of toys, and even my own bed. Although I prefer to sleep with mommy as I'm also her protector.

That night while lying in bed with mommy, she told me about all the wonderful adventures we would have. I told mommy about my nightmare and how I felt bad for those in the shelter. She said that's something I would never have to worry about, and we would find a way to help them.

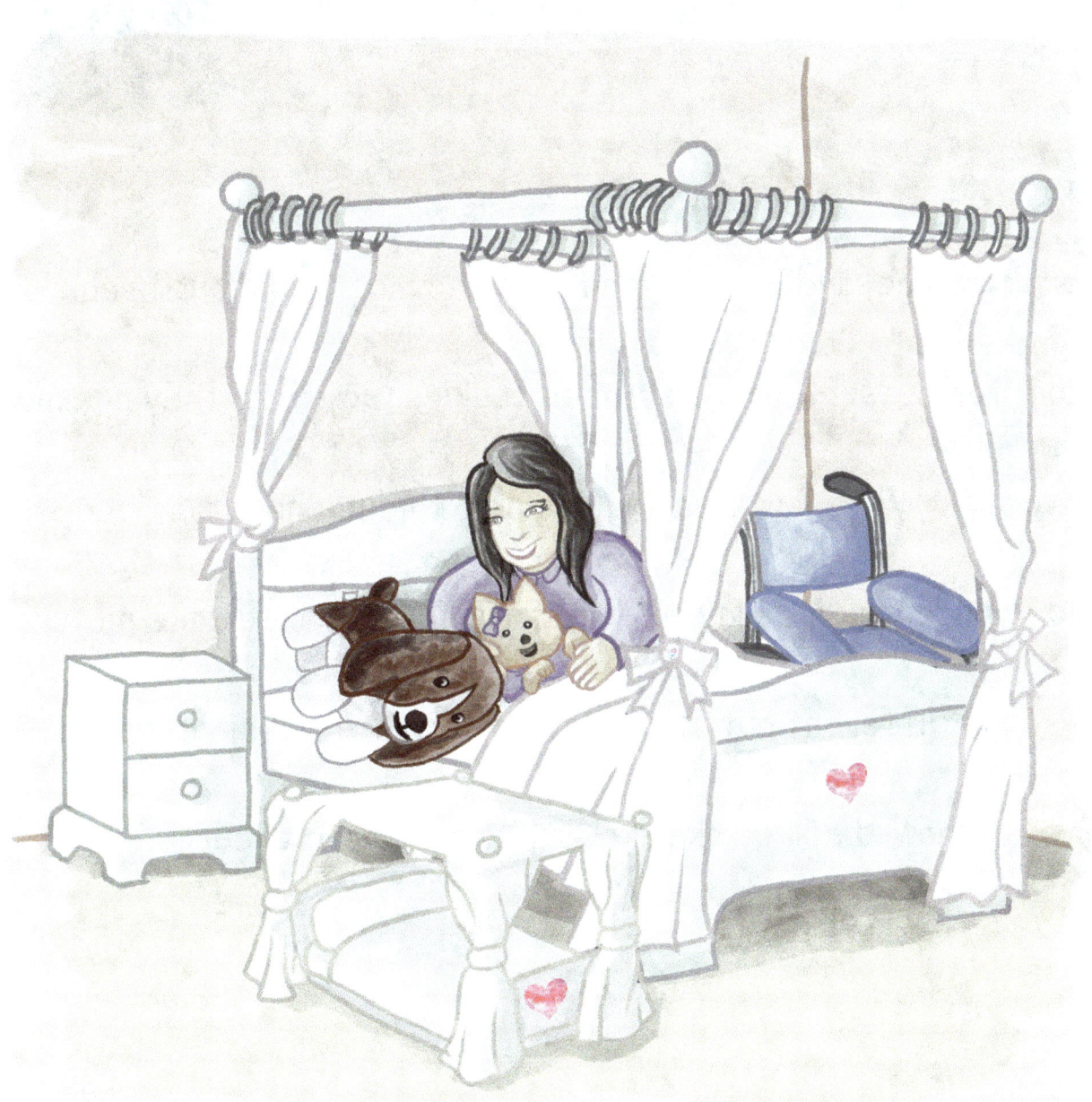

Morning came, and mommy made me the most delicious breakfast and, for dessert, peanut butter cookies. Boy, how they are my favorite. While I was eating, mommy told me about an idea she had. "Since you like playing dress-up, why don't we take pictures of you in different outfits and put them on a website." "This will show that it's okay to embrace our differences."

Mommy said this would take a lot of hard work, practice, and dedication for both of us. I assured mommy I was up for the challenge. It wasn't long before I had the most magnificent wardrobe. My closet was filled with beautiful dresses, hair bows, shoes, and amazing costumes of all kinds.

Mommy and I spent hours painting our nails, doing our hair, playing dress-up, creating scenes, and taking photos.

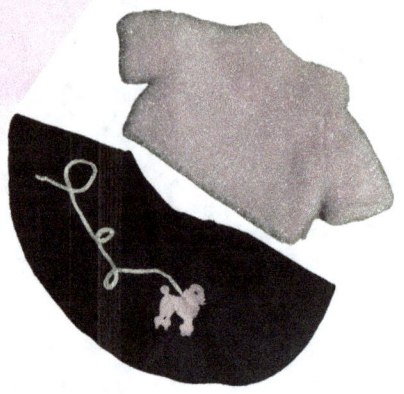

Soon our website was live. Before long, we were getting hundreds of thousands of views. People checked each week to see what new adventure we had.

People loved me so much that they would message mommy trying to buy me. Of course, mommy said no way. I asked mommy if they loved how different I was, then why didn't they adopt an animal from the shelter? Many like me need good homes. Mommy said, "that's a good question, and unfortunately, the shelter has a stigma of being something to be ashamed of

"This gave me an idea. Mommy, you are so good at taking pictures; why don't you visit the shelter and take photos of them for the website too? Mommy thought that was a great idea. She said she'd need my help because most animals can't talk like I can, and I would need to translate.

Soon our website was flooded with animals of all kinds. Unlike me, they didn't have happy homes or someone who loved them. This made the photos look sad. You really had to spend a lot of time cheering them up before we could get smiling pictures

Mommy then thought, "why don't we take the pictures of you and the animals at the shelter and put them on a calendar? Not only will the profits from the calendars help, but if people from the website want to see our new photos, they will have to go there and buy them." Off we were to have a meeting with animal control manager to make it happen.

Mommy has the best ideas. And so we got to work.

By the year's end, we had created the most fabulous calendars.

The shelter was flooded with people worldwide to buy the calendars on launch day—there were so many people in line they were wrapped outside around the building.

Manny of the helpers brought out animals for the people to play with while they waited.

The people soon realized that the animals from the shelter were much like me. While they may have only come for the calendars, they left with much more. By day's end, all the animals had been adopted, and funds to help many more.

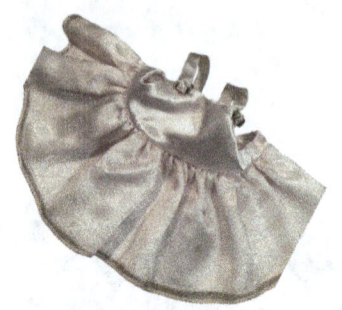

The best part is we are moving to a farm where we can help many more rescues recover and find their forever homes.

And the adventure continues!

Special Bonus

Foxey loved playing hide and seek. Every picture has one or more heart's hidden within the page. How many can you find?

Want to follow Foxey for more adventures find us at

Website www.foxeysfabulousadventures.com

Instagram @foxeysfabulousadventures

Facebook @foxeysfabulousadventures

Twitter @foxeysadventure

Coming Soon

www.ingramcontent.com/pod-product-compliance
Lightning Source LLC
Chambersburg PA
CBHW082022050526
44107CB00100B/602